Who Has Time for Hugs?

Shimoqua Thomas

ISBN: 978-1-945532-04-7

Illustrated by: Keira Laraque
Published by: Opportune Independent Publishing Company

For bulk orders, or author requests, contact Shimoqua Thomas directly at **contactme@isayahsworld.com** or visit **www.isayahsworld.com**.

Printed in the United States of America
For permission requests, write to the publisher, addressed "Attention: Permissions Coordinator," at the address below.

Info@opportunepublishing.com
www.opportunepublishing.com

Dedication

I dedicate this book to my first love, my mom, Matilda Thomas. You have shown me how to be the woman I am today. I only hope to make you proud. To my second love, my son. You inspire me to be a better version of myself everyday. You are my pride and joy, my everything. I am the lucky one. Thanks for choosing me to be your mom.

Rise and shine sleepy head!

Isayah, It's time to get out of bed.

"Can mommy have a hug?"

I have ducks to feed.

Big fast trains to lead.

And I am still learning how to potty.

You must run and jump to keep up with me.

I have so many places that I must be.

But first, can I help you make breakfast for me?

I have red balls to chase and two shoes to lace.

I have soft cats to pet and puddles of mud to jump over next.

Other kids will want to play. Oooh! I can't wait.

Mama, can we just hug another day?

There are cars to fix and
Play-Doh to squish.

Oh, Mama! Don't stop my fun.

There are so many things I
have to get done.

Today I can meet up with my friends.

They love playing games that never end.

They all hide behind trees, while I count 1, 2, 3...

There are so many adventures
to come.

Look, mama!

There is a big brown dog.

Can I have one?

With so many new words to say and new things to see, I will never stop learning.

Grandma and Grandpa would be so proud of me!

I'm going to say my ABC's and 123's.

This time I'll go all the way.

Mommy I know you are happy because I remember all the things you teach me everyday.

Tick Tock, Tick Tock

Do you hear the clock?

My eyes are getting heavy.

Is my bath water ready?

And where is my teddy?

The sun is gone and the day is done.

Here is my favorite book to read.

Mommy can you do one more thing for me?

Can I have a hug please?

www.ingramcontent.com/pod-product-compliance
Lightning Source LLC
Chambersburg PA
CBHW040022050426
42452CB00002B/93